A Humanist Funeral Service and Celebration

A Humanist Funeral Service and Celebration

CORLISS LAMONT

Revised by Beth K. Lamont and J. Sierra Oliva

 Prometheus Books

59 John Glenn Drive
Amherst, New York 14228–2119

Published 2011 by Prometheus Books

A Humanist Funeral Service and Celebration, Copyright © 1954, 1977 by Corliss Lamont. All rights reserved. Revised edition © 2011 by the Estate of Corliss Lamont. No part of this publication may be reproduced, stored in a retrieval system, or transmitted in any form or by any means, digital, electronic, mechanical, photocopying, recording, or otherwise, or conveyed via the Internet or a website without prior written permission of the publisher, except in the case of brief quotations embodied in critical articles and reviews.

Inquiries should be addressed to
Prometheus Books
59 John Glenn Drive
Amherst, New York 14228–2119
VOICE: 716–691–0133
FAX: 716–691–0137
WWW.PROMETHEUSBOOKS.COM

15   5 4 3

Library of Congress Cataloging-in-Publication Data

Lamont, Corliss, 1902–1995.
    A Humanist funeral service and celebration / by Corliss Lamont. — Rev. version / by J. Sierra Oliva.
       p. cm.
    Rev. ed. of: A Humanist funeral service.
    Includes bibliographical references.
    ISBN 978–1–61614–409–8 (pbk. : alk. paper)
    ISBN 978–1–61614–410–4 (e-book)
    1. Funeral service. 2. Humanism, Religious. I. Sierra-Oliva, Jesus. II. Lamont, Corliss, 1902–1995. Humanist funeral service. III. Title.

BL2777.B8L36 2011
203'.88—dc22

2011004169

Printed in the United States of America on acid-free paper

CONTENTS

Preface	7
Acknowledgments	11
Introductory Music	17
The Service	19
Burial Service	27
Service for a Child	31
Cremation Service	35
Service for Interment of Ashes	39
A Memorial Service	41
Additional Suggestions for Music	47
Additional Suggestions for Poetry	51

Preface

There has long been a widely felt need for a funeral service centering around a nonsupernatural, Humanist philosophy of existence. The Humanist view, stemming from some of the greatest thinkers in history, rejects the idea of personal immortality and interprets death as the final end of the individual conscious personality. The philosophy or religion of Humanism sets up the happiness and progress of humankind on this earth as the supreme goal of human endeavor.

Whatever changes may take place in our dynamic twenty-first-century society and whatever science may achieve in prolonging the average lifespan, we can be certain that human beings will always have to confront the major crisis of death. The stark fact of mortality will continue to evoke in the human heart dominant moods such as sorrow, tragedy, love, hope, resignation, and courage. And it seems probable that most people throughout the world will wish to maintain the tradition of some simple ceremony to express appreciation, grief, and farewell when a friend or relative dies.

A funeral service is, moreover, helpful in overcoming any sense of unreality about the death of a loved one. It brings out the finality of the parting with the person, the fact that past relationships with him or her have been severed and that a new relationship of memory alone must be established.

Rituals concerned with death are a form of art and should appeal to the aesthetic sense. In my opinion they ought to be dignified, brief, and reminiscent of the deep social ties in experience; they ought to avoid sentimentality, showiness, and somberness. But funeral services should not try to avoid stirring up the emotions. Psychological wisdom has clearly shown that the suppression of emotion in the face of death may have harmful consequences and that the normal expression of grief can serve as a healthy release and purge of tension.

With the inevitable misgivings of one who is exploring a subject that is both delicate and difficult, I am presenting a tentative version of a funeral service that may be considered appropriate by modern minds. Within the broad outlines of the Humanist worldview I have tried to stress three main points: humanity's kinship with Nature, the naturalness of death, and the far-reaching social interrelations and ideals of human living.

Those who make use of this service will, of course, feel free to alter it as they see fit, especially in regard to the selections of music and poetry. For here individual preference is of the greatest importance and the dead person's own favorites may well be the determining factor. I have appended at the end of this little book a number of alternate choices for music and poetry. I have likewise left it to individual taste to decide whether to include in the service biographical material and some sort of tribute to the deceased. I myself believe that in most cases a friend or member of the family should speak briefly about the life of the dead person and its significance.

This Humanist service appeared initially as an article in 1940 in *Unity*, a liberal religious magazine. It was first published in book form by The Beacon Press in 1947. In the light of criticisms made by ministers and other individuals, I have considerably revised and expanded this fourth edition. The service can function either as a regular funeral service prior to interment or cremation; or as a memorial service at some time subsequent to interment or cremation. For commitment to the earth or flames I have added special material.

As it stands at present, the service proper, not including possible biographical remarks, lasts a little more than twenty minutes, of which about half is taken up by the selections of music. The meditations and quoted passages of prose and poetry are to be read by the minister or whoever is in charge of the ceremony.

The quotation on page 21 is from Anne Parrish's novel *Golden Wedding*, Harper & Brothers, 1936, page 343.

New York City C.L.
January, 1977

I have added the term "celebration" to the title of this work to denote our celebration of the person's life.

San Diego J.S.O.
February 2011

Acknowledgments

The author and editor of this book wishes to thank the following publishers, agents or individuals, holding copyright on poems specified, for permission to reprint:

>The *Atlantic Monthly* for "Shelley's poems, 'He is made one with Nature.'"
>Joseph Auslander for "In Memoriam."
>Dodd, Mead & Company, Inc., for W. H. Mallock's translation of Lucretius; for Rupert Brooke's "The Dead," Sonnets III and IV from *The Collected Poems of Rupert Brooke*, copyright 1915;
>To Rabindranat Tagore for "Fruit Gathering."

Estate of A.E. Housman, through M.C.A. Management, Ltd. For "Parta Quies" from *More Poems* by A. E. Housman.

To Robert Louis Stevenson for "Requiem."

To Walt Whitman for his poem "When Lilacs Last Bloom'd in the Door Yard" –*Leaves of Grass*.

Harper & Brothers for "And You as Well Must Die, Beloved Dust," from *Second April* by Edna St. Vincent Millay, published by Harper & Brothers, copyright 1920, 1948 by Edna St. Vincent Millay.

Excerpt from "Heritage" reprinted with permission of the publisher from *An Act of Life* by Theodore Spencer, p. 34, Cambridge, Mass.: Harvard University Press, copyright © 1944 by the President and Fellows of Harvard College. Copyright renewed 1971 by Eloise Spencer Bender.

William Heinemann, Ltd., and Gabriel Wells for the excerpt from Algernon Charles Swinburne's "The Garden of Proserpine."

Alfred A. Knopf, Inc., for permission to reprint Sonnet XXVI from *Tumultuous Shore* by Arthur Davison Ficke, copyright 1942 by Arthur Davison Ficke.

The Macmillan Company for "Margaritae

Sorori" from *Collected Poems* by William Ernest Henley; for "A Loftier Race" by John Addington Symonds' for "The Choir Invisible" by George Eliot.

Charles Scribner's Sons for "To W. P." from *Poems* by George Santayana, copyright 1921 by George Santayana, copyright 1953 by Charles Scribner's Sons.

"Dear Lovely Death" from *The Collected Poems of Langston Hughes* by Langston Hughes, edited by Arnold Rampersad with David Roessel, associate editor, copyright © 1994 by the Estate of Langston Hughes. Used by permission of Alfred A. Knopf, a division of Random House, Inc.

A Humanist Funeral Service and Celebration

Introductory Music

It is usually desirable to have fifteen or twenty minutes of introductory music while people are gathering for the funeral service at the house, apartment, hall, or church. For the music an organ or piano is preferable. Instrumental or vocal accompaniment, if it can be arranged, naturally adds its own special quality. The playing of first-rate recordings can also be satisfactory. The following selections are suggested for the period prior to the service:

1. Handel's "Largo" from *Xerxes*
2. Gluck's "Dance of the Spirits" from *Orpheus*
3. Rubinstein's *Kamennoi Ostrov*
4. Bach's *Come Sweet Death*
5. Massenet's *Meditation and Elegie*

The Service

(There is to be a short pause between the introductory music and the service proper. The beginning of the service can be indicated by the person in charge taking his place.)

MUSIC: Beethoven's *Seventh Symphony*, Second Movement, first third.

INTRODUCTION: We are gathered here today to do honor to the life and memory of _____. Death has come to our friend, as it comes eventually to all human beings.

MEDITATION: The occurrence of death brings home to us the common concerns, the common crises, and the common destiny of all who live upon this earth. Death draws us together in the deep-felt emotions of the heart; it dramatically accents the ultimate equality involved in our ultimate fate; it reminds us of the essential brotherhood of Humanity that lies beneath all the bitter dissensions and divisions registered in history and contemporary affairs. The human race, with its infinite roots reaching back over the boundless past and its infinite ramifications extending throughout the present world and ever pushing forward into the future, is one great family. The living and the dead and the generations yet unborn make up that enduring communion of humanity, which shares the adventure of life upon this dear and pleasant earth.

Here on our planet there have evolved, over millions of years, human beings possessed of the power of mind, the beauty of love, the splendor of heroism. Men and women, with all their diverse gifts, are fully part and product of the Nature that is their home. They are cousins to all other living forms; and in their very flesh and blood one with that same marvelous and multistructured matter that underlies the whole mighty universe, the shining array of stars, the gracious sun, our own world and everything within it.

This great and eternal Nature it is in which we ever live and move and have our being. Thus, beyond our kinship with our fellow men, there is always our kinship with the natural world that sustains us with its varied goods and stirs us with its wonderful beauty. This dynamic Nature stamps its pattern of constant change on every existing thing. Change means transformation, beginnings, and endings; birth, growth, and death. So it is that the freshness and delight of each new day, the continual zest of living, are tempered by the sting of transiency.

Yet transiency and death itself are entirely natural and understandable in our universe. Life and death are different and essential aspects of the same creative process. It is Nature's law that living organisms should eventually retire from the scene and so make way for newborn generations. In this sense life affirms itself *through* death. Each one of us "must die for the sake of life, for the flow of the stream too great to be dammed in any pool, for the growth of the seed too strong to stay in one shape. . . . Because these bodies must perish we are greater than we know." In the larger view, then in the total picture, death as such is not an evil and is not to be feared by reasoning people.

We recognize these truths. And we accept as inevitable the eventual extinction of human individuals and the return of their bodies, indestructible in their ultimate elements, to the Nature that brought them forth. *In death, as in life, we belong to Nature.*

MUSIC: Grieg's "Morning" from *The Peer Gynt Suite.*

MEDITATION: Although it is premature death that is most tragic, the final parting signified by death is bound to bring shock and sorrow whenever the ties of love and friendship are involved. Those who feel deeply will grieve deeply. No philosophy or religion ever taught can prevent this wholly natural reaction of the human heart.

Whatever relationships and enterprises death breaks in upon, we can be sure that those whom we have lost are finally and eternally at peace. And whatever length of time we have had a friend, we always remain grateful for his having lived and for our having known him in the full richness of his personality.

Nothing now can detract from the joy and beauty that we shared with _____; nothing can possibly affect the happiness and depth of experience that he himself knew. What has been, has been—forever. The past, with all its meaning, is sacred and secure. Our love for him and his love for us, his family and friends, cannot be altered by time or circumstance.

We rejoice that _____ was and is a part of our lives. (We rejoice that he lives on in our minds.) His influence endures in the unending consequences flowing from his character and deeds; it endures in our own acts and thoughts. We shall remember him as a living, vital presence. That memory will bring refreshment to our hearts and strengthen us in time. These are reflections that we treasure; for there can never be too much friendship in the world, too much human warmth, too much love.

And what is love? Love is life. It gives life and protects life.

BRIEF PERSONAL REMARKS or TRIBUTES. (Optional.)

MEDITATION: On this occasion, as we reflect upon human existence and its meaning, it is for us, the living, to dedicate ourselves anew to those great ethical aims and ideals that have long been part of our Humanist heritage; to reaffirm that friendliness and sympathy toward our fellow human beings, which now, as always, remain the foundation-stone of a good society; to resolve anew to bend our minds and energies toward the pursuit of truth, the creation of beauty, and the advancement of freedom. Beyond the welfare of our native land, we look to the world at large and seek the happiness and progress of all humanity upon this fruitful earth—to the end that everywhere men and women enjoy life more abundantly.

May the human race ever flourish, ever grow in grace and wisdom and generosity. May generation after generation through eternities of time come to know the sweetness of living and rejoice in the inexhaustible beauties of this universe of Nature.

In Humanism we recognize that it was Nature's processes that gave existence to all of us. That is why Humanists respect Nature and honor Humanity.

Nature aids us through other humans. And they are the only help we have to help us survive on this planet. And we must honor those who help us withstand the vicissitudes of life, and make us happy with their love.

When those who gave us birth and guided us or loved and befriended us die, we are devastated and suffer and cry; but like today, we can also rejoice with their memory, their legacy, and their fruitful acts of love.

MUSIC: Brahms's *First Symphony*, Fourth Movement, first third.

ANNOUNCEMENT: The service is concluded. Interment (or commitment) will be private.

MUSIC: (Optional. About five minutes of additional music may be played while the people are leaving.)

Burial Service

(This service is designed to take place at the grave, after the coffin has been lowered. Two forms of service are here suggested, the second being for a person comparatively young at the time of his death.)

I

In committing the body of _____ to this hallowed ground, we do so with deep respect for the remains of the person, who showed a unique and beloved personality. And we think of the words of Socrates, "that no evil can befall a good man in life or after death."

Here, under the wide and open sky, our friend

will rest in peace. We dedicate this simple plot, amid these natural surroundings, to every beautiful and precious memory associated with him.

We lay his body in that gentle earth that has been the chief support of Humankind since first he walked beneath the sun. To all human beings, to all living forms, the soil has ever provided the sustenance that is the staff of life. To that good earth we now give back the body of our friend and say with the poet Shelley:

> He is made one with Nature: there is heard
> His voice to all her music, from the moan
> Of thunder, to the song of night's sweet bird.
> He is a presence to be felt and known
> In darkness and in light, from herb and stone
> He is a portion of the loveliness
> Which once he made more lovely . . .

II

For the Young

In saying our last farewell to_____, we shall read a sonnet by George Santayana, who once wrote: "The length of things is vanity; only their height is joy."

READING: From Santayana's *To W. P.*

With you a part of me hath passed away;
For in the peopled forest of my mind
A tree made leafless by this wintry wind
Shall never don again its green array.
Chapel and fireside, country road and bay,
Have something of their friendliness resigned;
Another, if I would, I could not find,
And I am grown much older in a day.
But yet I treasure in my memory
Your gift of charity, your mellow ease,
And the dear honor of your amity;
For these once mine, my life is rich with these.
And I scarce know which part may greater be,—
What I keep of you, or you rob from me.

III

In committing the body of _____ to this hallowed ground, we do so with deep reverence for that body as the temple, during life, of a unique and beloved personality. Here, under the wide and open sky, our friend will rest in peace. And we dedicate this simple plot, amid these natural surroundings, to every beautiful and precious memory associated with him.

We lay his body in that gentle earth that has

been the chief support of Humankind since it walked beneath the sun. To all human beings, to all living forms, the soil has ever provided the sustenance that is the staff of life. To the good earth and to the great Nature that is the source of human existence, we now give back the body of our friend, with the full and certain knowledge that, in the words of Socrates, "no evil can befall a good man in life or after death."

Service for a Child

*D*ear Folks, for all of us who are gathered together today to lay to rest the tiniest among us, there is no way in the world to offer comfort: not to the parents, not to the relatives, not to the friends.

Our grief is truly inconsolable. We who demand logical explanations are at a complete loss in what seems to be the total caprice and indifference of any just-powers that be, or any hope for good will in the world. It leaves us angry, bewildered, and inconsolable.

We feel helpless in the face of this needless, pointless snuffing-out of a beautiful little life that had just barely begun. For the short time he/she was with us, think of the joy and wonderment that we experienced. We're thinking of all of the joy and wonderment that this little one would have experienced in a normal lifetime, now never to be known. What a tragic loss.

As people of good will ourselves, who reach out to others in loving ways, this amounts to what seems to be an outright betrayal, by Nature itself, of the benevolent forces we would wish to have prevail in our world.

There is no way that we can accept this tragedy, or even to breathe a sigh of resignation, or to say those traditional, mythical things about god's will, or to be comforted, that this dear child is safe with the angels now.

And, perhaps our grief is even compounded because we are Freethinkers—we are moderns— with our demand for logic in the universe, and for the use of reason in dealing with our daily lives. This leaves us bare-naked, unclothed by the illusion of immortality, and its comforting illogic. Maybe we even doubt our own convictions that our human life here on earth is enough.

So, let us do what we humans do best: comfort each other! A psychologist stated that in order to be emotionally healthy that we humans need at least four hugs a day. What a lovely formula! Would that each of us in this world were so lucky. But, in honor of our little one, who will not be able to give and receive these hugs, which in an average lifetime of seventy-five years, might amount to at least umpteen zillion hugs, we might dedicate our own love, and proceed to deliver these hugs ourselves on her/his behalf.

Let us who wish to make this dedication begin with hugs for your neighbors sitting on either side of you. Then, please carry on . . . forever?

This is part of the philosophy of Humanist Healing for the Woes of the World . . . that of reaching out to each other. May this give some bit of comfort in our grievous loss today. Thank you for being here and please feel free now to share your own feelings with each other as well.

Cremation Service

(This service is designed to take place in the anteroom or chapel of the crematorium, just before the cremation itself. Two forms of service are here suggested, the second being for a person comparatively young at the time of his death.)

I

In committing the body of _____ to the flames, we do so with deep respect for the remains of a Humanist who had a unique and beloved personality. Through the purifying process of fire this body now becomes transformed into the more simple and ultimate elements of our universe. Fire is itself one of the great forces of Nature.

READING: From *Fruit-Gathering* by Sir Rabindranath Tagore:

O Fire, my brother, I sing victory to you.
You are the bright red image of fearful freedom.
You swing your arms in the sky, you sweep your impetuous fingers across the harp-string, your dance music is beautiful . . .
My body will be one with you, my heart will be caught in the whirls of your frenzy, and the burning heat that was my life will flash up and mingle itself in your flame.

To this same flame, then, we give finally the body of our friend, with the full and certain knowledge that, in the words of Socrates, "not even fire can obliterate a good person's memory."

II

For the Young

In saying our last farewell to _____, we shall read a sonnet by George Santayana, who once wrote: "The length of things is vanity, only their height is joy."

READING: From Santayana's *To W. P.*

With you a part of me hath passed away;
For in the peopled forest of my mind
A tree made leafless by this wintry wind
Shall never don again its green array.
Chapel and fireside, country road and bay,
Have something of their friendliness resigned;
Another, if I would, I could not find,
And I am grown much older in a day.
But yet I treasure in my memory
Your gift of charity, your mellow ease,
And the dear honor of your amity;
For these once mine, my life is rich with these.
And I scarce know which part may greater be,—
What I keep of you, or you rob from me.

In committing the body of _____ to the flames, we do so with deep respect for the remains of a young person who in life had a unique and beloved personality. Through the purifying process of fire this body now becomes transformed into the more simple and ultimate elements of our universe. Fire is itself one of the great forces of Nature. In the heavens above it shines out with majestic splendor in the warming and life-giving sun and in all the infinite host of stars; upon our earth it is the versatile servant of humankind and one of the bases of civilization.

To this same fire, then, we give finally the body of our friend, with the full and certain knowledge that, in the words of Socrates, "no evil can befall a good man in life or after death."

SERVICE FOR INTERMENT OF ASHES

(If the ashes are interred in a burial plot, the family may wish to have a further brief ceremony such as the following.)

In placing the ashes of _____ in this hallowed ground, we think again of all that our dear companion and friend meant and means to us. And we dedicate this simple plot, amid these natural surroundings, to every beautiful and precious memory associated with him/her.

We lay these ashes in that gentle earth that has been the chief support of humankind since first it walked beneath the sun. To all human beings, to all living forms, the soil has ever provided the sustenance that is the staff of life. To that good earth we now commit the ashes of our friend and say with the poet Shelley:

> He is made one with Nature: there is heard
> His voice to all her music, from the moan
> Of thunder, to the song of night's sweet bird.
> He is a presence to be felt and known
> In darkness and in light, from herb and stone
> He is a portion of the loveliness
> Which once he made more lovely . . .

A Memorial Service

Order of Ceremony:

1. Introductory Music
2. Words of Welcome
3. Thoughts on Life and Death from a Humanist perspective
4. The Tribute—An outline of the life and personality of ———
5. Readings of Appropriate Poetry or Prose
6. Remarks from Family and Friends
7. Private Reflections Accompanied by Music
8. Closing words

We are here for a sad occasion; the loss of a friend and family member. We would prefer to make this a remembrance and a celebration of the life of ————. We need to turn this moment around to emphasize, not our loss, but that which we can keep forever; something precious that nothing and no one can take away from us: those personal memories that belong to us. We had the privilege of knowing this lovely person and sharing our world with her, and she, sharing her world with us, if only for too brief a time.

———— asked to be remembered in a nonreligious or Humanist ceremony. She felt that this life is enough, without a promise of a reward elsewhere, and without some kind of supernatural intervention. She didn't feel the need to reach out to make a connection with traditional promises of a paradise in another world.

She was aware, as each of us is, that life is all too short, this brief time in the sunshine between the two mysterious darknesses, those shadowed areas of our coming-into-being and of going-out-of-being. She knew, as most of us know, that the very fragility of life, even the precariousness of living, makes each human life even that much more precious. Humanists are so acutely aware of our mortality.

We accept the responsibility, as ———— did, while we can enjoy being alive, of trying, in whatever way we can, to give joy to others, and to make this earthly existence tolerable, or at least as close as we can get it to the idealized concept of a mythical heaven; that is, living in peace and harmony with our fellow humans, finding an earthly reward in all of our endeavors, in our communities, in our homes, and in the sharing of compassionate, positive, productive, and loving relationships with our friends and family.

Each of us confronts death in our own way. Each of us grieves in our own time. Each of us faces the reality of this irrevocable loss differently. No one set of words or rituals will speak to us as we journey through our personal grief. Yet, words and rituals are all we have. Limited, perhaps, words afford us the opportunity to give voice to the tangle of feelings that dwell deep within us. Sometimes collected readings, reflecting these diverse thoughts that deal with the wide range of questions and emotions that we experience in our grief, can bring some comfort by bringing into focus new dimensions that may have eluded us. That's what words of poetry and inspiration are all about.

All of us here have been touched by death. What are we to do? How is it possible to comfort one another when all of us are overwhelmed by pain and sorrow? Where do we turn? Who will hold us and give us strength? This is when it is most important to turn to each other. It is almost like we are groping in the darkness, unsure of our path. In the darkness of this night, in the depth of our dispair, we reach out to each other. Though weakened, joining together gives us strength and courage and hope and knowledge that together, friend supporting friend, we will journey through the darkness to find the light of another day.

When we come to grieve at the loss of a friend or family member, we face also, thoughts of our own demise. It is almost impossible to imaging NOT being. We can identify with sleeping, immersed in an unconscious world, and then, of course, waking! But to NOT waken seems so frightening. In dealing with this thought as a teen, when the reality of the finality of death was giving me panic attacks, I began to comfort myself with a little made-up verse that went like this: Before I was, I knew no pain; not being will take me there again.

It is easy to understand why the primitives expected that the breath that made life possible was one and the same with the concept of spirit. And when the lifebreath escaped the body for the last time, it would go to another place where spirits dwelled. This has been a comfort in traditional beliefs. But ——— recognized the capriciousness of that mythical being in a spirit world that promises everlasting life. This is the same mythical being that belief in which can pit human beings against each other in wars of vengeance, and in its myriad incarnations, has wreaked havoc with the people of this beautiful Planet Earth.

———'s wish to have a Humanist remembrance ceremony shows her faith in something more tangible: that humans can manage their own lives in a rational and ethical manner. This is consistent with the Humanist philosophy that believes we humans have evolved and are still evolving. There'll come a time when we've all outgrown the fairytales of childhood, and get on to the business of being adults, responsible for, and improving, our human condition. Humanists say that we work for peace on earth because we have no place else to go! We have no escape hatch to bail us out of the mess we've made of our human home. As for this sense of responsibility: if there's no one "upstairs," who listens to prayers, who then will answer? We must!

What is truly lasting, and truly lives beyond us, in addition to other people's memories of us, is the good works that we do in our lifetime, in our interactions with others, and with the world around us. The cumulative good works that ——— has done in her lifetime has added to the wealth of our own being.

Here are comforting words: There are stars whose radiance is visible on earth, though they have long been extinct. There are people whose brilliance continues to light the world though they are no longer among the living. So it may be with your loved one: though she no longer walks among us, may her light continue to shine within the world. May her memory illumine those who love her, continuing to strengthen them throughout their lives.

We belong to the earth, and we return to the earth. Here is a thought about the cycle in harmony with nature:

> To Nature's tree what's left of me,
> my ashes you must bring,
> And scatter wide to seep inside the ground
> beneath her feet,
> That I who cried for life denied,
> found suddenly so sweet, might
> Live, if only for, a moment more,
> some lovely newborn spring.
>
> Beth K. Lamont

Perhaps those of you gathered here would like to share your remembrances of ———. Please feel free to come to the mike so that we can all hear of these memories.

Additional Suggestions for Music

*I*n selecting and suggesting music for a humanist funeral service, I have tried to choose pieces that are dignified and serene, though not necessarily ones composed with the theme of death in mind. I include some well-known examples of professional funeral music, though a good deal of such music seems to me too dramatic, powerful, or solemn for the type of service I have written.

There are also included a few selections of Nature music, since the music that comes in toward the middle of the service is meant to suggest the beauty and splendor of Nature, Humanity's sole and sufficient home.

Most of the pieces mentioned are available in scores for both piano and organ. It is comparatively easy for a trained musician to transcribe piano into organ music where that may be necessary. In presenting the following additional selections for music, I do not, of course, pretend to have exhausted the possibilities:

Bach, "Sonatina" from *Cantata 106*
Beethoven, "Adagio" from *Piano Concerto No. 4*
Brahms, *A German Requiem*, first fourth
Chopin, *Marche Funebre*
Debussy, *Clair de Lune*
Delius, *Over the Hills and Far Away*, opening part
Dvorak, *Fifth Symphony* (from *The New World*), Second Movement, first third
Dvorak, *Song My Mother Taught Me*
Faure, *Plaisir d'Amour*
Grieg, *The Last Spring*
Handel, "Dead March" from *Saul*
Kern, "Wandering Westward" from *Mark Twain*
Kreisler, *Liebesleid*
MacDowell, "To a Wild Rose" from *Woodland Sketches*
Mascagni, "Intermezzo" from *Cavaleria Rusticana*

Mozart, Funeral Masonic Music/Adagio Violin Concert 2
Pachelbel, *Canon*
Ravel, *Pavane for a Dead Princess*
Schubert, *Death and the Maiden*, Second Movement
Wagner, "Liebestod" from *Tristan and Isolde*

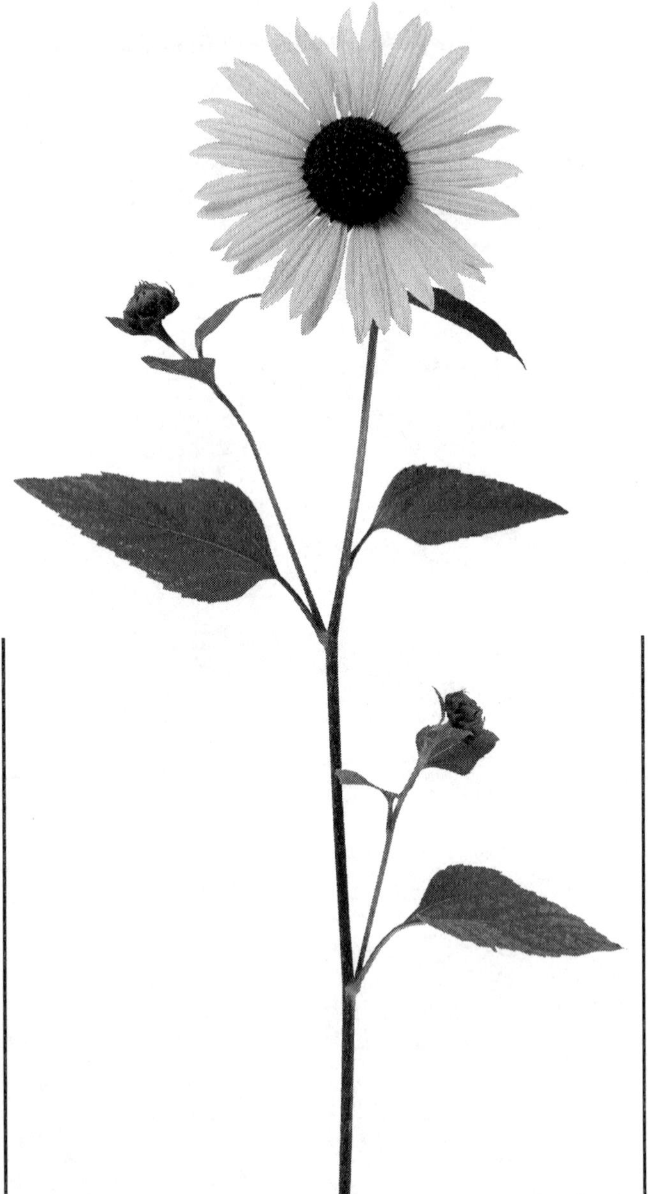

Additional Suggestions for Poetry

Death has always been one of the great themes for poets of every age and country. And there are a vast number of poems about death that embody a Humanist viewpoint. For inclusion here I have chosen various outstanding poems that give expression to some aspect of the Humanist philosophy and that are appropriate for reading aloud at a Humanist funeral service or meeting.

And If He Die?

And if he die? He for an hour has been
Alive, aware of what it is, to be.
The high majestic hills, the shining sea,
He has looked upon, and meadows golden-green.
The stars in all their glory he has seen.
Love he has felt. This poor dust that is he
Has stirred with pulse of inward liberty,
And touched the extremes of hope, and all
  between.
Can the small pain of death-beds, can the sting
Of parting from the accustomed haunts of earth,
Make him forget the bounty of his birth
And cancel out his grateful wondering
That he has known exultance and the worth
Of being himself a song the dark powers sing?

Arthur Davison Ficke

In Memoriam

They are not dead, our sons who fell in glory,
Who gave their lives for Freedom and for Truth;
We shall grow old, but never their great story,
Never their gallant youth.

In a perpetual springtime set apart,
Their memory forever green shall grow,
In some bright secret meadow of the heart
Where never falls the snow.

Joseph Auslander

The Dead

I

Blow out, you bugles, over the rich Dead!
    There's none of these so lonely and poor of
       old,
    But, dying, has made us rarer gifts than gold.
These laid the world away; poured out the red
Sweet wine of youth; gave up the years to be
    Of work and joy, and that unhoped serene,
    That men call age; and those who would have
       been,
Their sons, they gave, their immortality.

Blow, bugles, blow! They brought us, for our
   dearth,
    Holiness, lacked so long, and Love, and Pain.
Honor has come back, as a king, to earth,
    And paid his subjects with a royal wage;
And Nobleness walks in our ways again;
    And we have come into our heritage.

II

These hearts were woven of human joys and cares,
   Washed marvelously with sorrow, swift to
      mirth.
The years had given them kindness. Dawn was
   theirs,
   And sunset, and the colors of the earth.
These had seen movement, and heard music; known
   Slumber and waking; loved; gone proudly
      friended;
Felt the quick stir of wonder; sat alone;
   Touched flowers and furs and cheeks. All this
      is ended.

There are waters blown by changing winds to
   laughter
And lit by the rich skies, all day. And after,
   Frost, with a gesture, stays the waves that
      dance
And wandering loveliness. He leaves a white
   Unbroken glory, a gathered radiance,
A width, a shining peace, under the night.

Rupert Brooke

Requiem

Under the wide and starry sky,
Dig the grave and let me lie:
Glad did I live and gladly die,
    And I laid me down with a will.

This be the verse you grave for me:
Here he lies where he longed to be;
Home is the sailor, home from the sea,
    And the hunter home from the hill.

Robert Louis Stevenson

From On the Nature of Things, Book III

No single thing abides; but all things flow.
Fragment to fragment clings—the things thus grow
    Until we know and name them. By degrees
They melt, and are no more the things we know.

Globed from the atoms falling slow or swift
I see the suns, I see the systems lift
    Their forms; and even the systems and the
        suns
Shall go back slowly to the eternal drift.

Thou too, oh earth—thine empires, lands, and
   seas—
Least, with thy stars, of all the galaxies,
   Globed from the drift like these, like these thou
      too
Shalt go. Thou art going, hour by hour, like these.

Nothing abides. Thy seas in delicate haze
Go off; those moonéd sands forsake their place;
   And where they are, shall other seas in turn
Mow with their scythes of whiteness other bays....

The seeds that once were we take flight and fly,
Winnowed to earth, or whirled along the sky,
   Not lost but disunited. Life lives on.
It is the lives, the lives, the lives, that die.

They go beyond recapture and recall,
Lost in the all-indissoluble All:—
   Gone like the rainbow from the fountain's
      foam,
Gone like the spindrift shuddering down the squall.

Flakes of the water, on the waters cease!
Soul of the body, melt and sleep like these.
   Atoms to Atoms—weariness to rest—
Ashes to ashes—hopes and fears to peace!

O Science, lift aloud thy voice that stills
The pulse of fear, and through the conscience thrills—
    Thrills through the conscience with the news
        of peace—
How beautiful thy feet are on the hills!

                              Lucretius
                         (Translated by W. H. Mallock)

Sonnet

And you as well must die, belovèd dust,
And all your beauty stand you in no stead;
This flawless, vital hand, this perfect head
This body of flame and steel, before the gust
Of Death, or under his autumnal frost,
Shall be as any leaf, be no less dead
Than the first leaf that fell,—this wonder fled
Altered, estranged, disintegrated, lost.
Nor shall my love avail you in your hour.
In spite of all my love, you will arise
Upon that day and wander down the air
Obscurely as the unattended flower,
It mattering not how beautiful you were,
Or how belovèd above all else.

                              Edna St. Vincent Millay

From The Garden of Proserpine

We are not sure of sorrow,
    And joy was never sure;
Today will die tomorrow,
    Time stoops to no man's lure;
And love, grown faint and fretful,
With lips but half regretful
Sighs, and with eyes forgetful
    Weeps that no loves endure.

From too much love of living,
    From hope and fear set free,
We thank with brief thanksgiving
    Whatever gods may be
That no life lives for ever;
That dead men rise up never;
That even the weariest river
    Winds somewhere safe to sea.

Then star nor sun shall waken,
    Nor any change of light:
Nor sound of waters shaken,
    Nor any sound or sight:
Nor wintry leaves nor vernal,
Nor days nor things diurnal;
Only the sleep eternal
    In an eternal night.

Algernon Charles Swinburne

From **When Lilacs Last in the Dooryard Bloom'd**

Come, lovely and soothing Death,
Undulate round the world, serenely arriving, arriving,
In the day, in the night, to all, to each,
Sooner or later, delicate death.

Prais'd be the fathomless universe,
For life and joy, and for objects and knowledge curious;
And for love, sweet love—but praise! praise! praise!
For the sure-enwinding arms of cool-enfolding Death.

Dark Mother, always gliding near, with soft feet,
Have none chanted for thee a chant of fullest welcome?
Then I chant it for thee—I glorify thee above all;
I bring thee a song that when thou must indeed come, come unfalteringly.

Approach, strong Deliveress!
When it is so—when thou hast taken them, I joyously sing the dead,
Lost in the loving, floating ocean of thee,
Laved in the flood of thy bliss, O Death.

From me to thee glad serenades,
Dances for thee I propose, saluting thee—
　adornments and feastings for thee;
And the sights of the open landscape, and the
　high-spread sky, are fitting,
And life and the fields, and the huge and
　thoughtful night.

The night in silence, under many a star;
The ocean shore, and the husky whispering wave,
　whose voice I know;
And the soul turning to thee, O vast and well-
　veil'd Death,
And the body gratefully nestling close to thee.

Over the tree-tops I float thee a song!
Over the rising and sinking waves—over the
　myriad fields, and the prairies wide;
Over the dense-pack'd cities all, and the teeming
　wharves and ways,
I float this carol with joy, with joy to thee,
　O Death!

Walt Whitman

Margaritae Sorori

A late lark twitters from the quiet skies;
And from the west,
Where the sun, his day's work ended,
Lingers as in content,
There falls on the old, gray city
An influence luminous and serene,
A shining peace.

The smoke ascends
In a rosy-and-golden haze. The spires
Shine and are changed. In the valley
Shadows rise. The lark sings on. The sun,
Closing his benediction,
Sinks, and the darkening air
Thrills with a sense of the triumphing night—
Night with her train of stars
And her great gift of sleep.

So be my passing!
My task accomplish'd and the long day done,
My wages taken, and in my heart
Some late lark singing,
Let me be gather'd to the quiet west,
The sundown splendid and serene,
Death.

William Ernest Henley

A Loftier Race

These things shall be,—a loftier race
    Than e'er the world hath known shall rise
With flame of freedom in their souls,
    And light of knowledge in their eyes.

They shall be gentle, brave, and strong
    To spill no drop of blood, but dare
All that may plant man's lordship firm
    On earth, and fire, and sea, and air.

They shall be simple in their homes,
    And splendid in their public ways,
Filling the mansions of the state
    With music and with hymns of praise.
Nation with nation, land with land,
    Unarmed shall live as comrades *free*;
In every heart and brain shall throb
    The pulse of one fraternity.

New arts shall bloom of loftier mould,
    And mightier music thrill the skies,
And every life shall be a song
    When all the earth is paradise.

John Addington Symonds

This is the same Humanist vision of Walt Whitman in "Joy Shipman Joy!"

The Choir Invisible

Oh may I join the choir invisible
Of those immortal dead who live again
In minds made better by their presence: live
In pulses stirred to generosity,
In deeds of daring rectitude, in scorn
For miserable aims that end with self,
In thoughts sublime that pierce the night like stars,
And with their mild persistence urge man's search
To vaster issues.

    So to live is heaven:
To make undying music in the world,
Breathing as beauteous order that controls
With growing sway the growing life of man.
So we inherit that sweet purity
For which we struggled, failed, and agonized
With widening retrospect that bred despair.
Rebellious flesh that would not be subdued,
A vicious parent shaming still its child,
Poor anxious penitence, is quick dissolved;
Its discords, quenched by meeting harmonies,
Die in the large and charitable air.
And all our rarer, better, truer self,
That sobbed religiously in yearning song,
That watched to ease the burden of the world,
Laboriously tracing what must be,
And what may yet be better—saw within

A worthier image for the sanctuary
And shaped it forth before the multitude,
Divinely human, raising worship so
To higher reverence more mixed with love—
That better self shall live til human Time
Shall fold its eyelids, and the human sky
Be gathered like a scroll within the tomb
Unread for ever.

          This is life to come,
Which martyred men have made more glorious
For us who strive to follow. May I reach
That purest heaven, be to other souls
The cup of strength in some great agony,
Enkindle generous ardor, feed pure love,
Beget the smiles that have no cruelty—
Be the sweet presence of a good diffused,
And in diffusion ever more intense.
So shall I join the choir invisible
Whose music is the gladness of the world.

George Eliot

From **Heritage**

What fills the heart of man
Is not that his life must fade,
But that out of his dark there can
A light like a rose be made,
That seeing a snow-flake fall
His heart is lifted up,
That hearing a meadow-lark call
For a moment he will stop
To rejoice in the musical air
To delight in the fertile earth
And the flourishing everywhere
Of spring and spring's rebirth.
And never a woman or man
Walked through their quickening hours
But found for some brief span
An intervale of flowers,
Where love for a man or woman
So captured the heart's beat
That they and all things human
Danced on rapturous feet.
And though, for each man, love dies,
And the rose has flowered in vain,
The rose to his children's eyes
Will flower again, again,
Will flower again out of shadow
To make the brief heart sing,

And the meadow-lark from the meadow
Will call again in spring.

         Theodore Spencer

Dear Lovely Death

Dear lovely Death
That taketh all things under wing—
Never to kill—
Only to change
Into some other thing
This suffering flesh,
To make it either more or less,
But not again the same—
Dear lovely Death,
Change is thy other name.

         Langston Hughes

On His Seventy-Fifth Birthday

I strove with none, for none was worth my strife.
Nature I loved and, next to Nature, Art:
I warmed both hands before the fire of life;
It sinks, and I am ready to depart.

         Walter Savage Landor